307
0

Northborough C.P. School,
Church Street,
Northborough,
Peterborough.

Going places available in hardback
People at work
How places change
Finding the way
People on holiday

Going places available in paperback
Town and countryside
Where people shop
People on the move
People at work

Acknowledgements

Illustrations by Tessa Richardson-Jones
Photographs by Zul Mukhida except for: pp. 6, 8bl, 14t,15, 20
Jenny Matthews; pp. 8t Bob Brecher, 8br Jayne Knights, 14bl Tim
Garrod, 24t John Heinrick, Zul Colour Library; pp. 10t Ancient Art and
Architecture Collection; p. 10b Museum of London; p. 11 E. T. Archive; p.
16 Robin Jackson; p. 19 Paul Harmer; p. 24m Mark Edwards, Still
Pictures; p. 24b Elanor Jackson; p. 26b Lupe Cunha Photos; p. 27 Leslie
Woodhead, Hutchison Library.

The author and publisher would like to thank the staff and pupils
of Balfour Infant School, Brighton.

A CIP catalogue record for this book is available from
the British Library.

ISBN 0-7136-5937-8

First paperback edition published 2001
First published in hardback in 1994 by
A & C Black (Publishers) Ltd
37 Soho Square, London, W1D 3QZ
© 1994 A & C Black (Publishers) Ltd

A CIP record for this book is available from
the British Library.

Typeset by Rowland Phototypesetting Ltd,
Bury St Edmunds, Suffolk
Printed in Belgium by Proost International Book Production

going places

Town and countryside

Barbara Taylor

Illustrations by Tessa Richardson-Jones
Photographs by Zul Mukhida and Jenny Matthews

Contents

A & C Black · London

Small villages, big towns

Do you live in a town, a city or a village in the countryside?

Nearly half of all the people in the world live in or around towns or cities. They are surrounded by houses, shops, offices and busy streets.

In the countryside, people live in small clusters of buildings called villages, which are spaced out among fields and woods. These people can enjoy peaceful surroundings but they have to travel to a nearby town to buy many of the things they need.

What do you think are the differences between living in a busy town or city and living in the countryside?

There's lots of things to see and do in a city.

There's plenty of places to walk and cycle in the countryside.

Which of the pictures around the edge of the page show life in the country? Which show life in a town? Can you think of three things which are the same in the town and in the country?

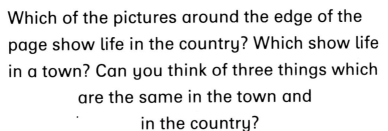

Look carefully at these photographs of towns and villages in other parts of the world. What do you think it would be like to live in these places? Think about the size of each place, how people might travel around and whether the place looks quiet and peaceful or busy and noisy.

Jaiselmer, India

Mont St Michel, France

Village homes in Malawi

Imagine you have a friend who lives in another part of the country. How could you tell them about your school and the place you live in? You could write them a letter or draw a plan of your local area to point out the main features.

What questions would you ask your friend about their town or village? Here are some ideas.

How do you get to school?

Where do you go shopping?

What do you do at the weekend?

Is there a lot of traffic near your home?

What do you do at school all day?

How towns began

Many thousands of years ago, people did not live in villages or towns. Most of the time they wandered from place to place, often sheltering in caves. They hunted wild animals, fished and gathered roots and berries to eat.

Cave people painted pictures on cave walls of the animals they hunted. This cave painting of a bull is about 17,000 years old.

This is how we think people in Britain lived about 2,000 years ago. Early settlements were built in safe places which had rich farmland.

Gradually, as people learned to tame animals and farm the land, they began to settle and build homes. Their animals provided them with meat, milk and wool, and carried heavy loads.

This painting shows people mining coal in 1544. Where do you think the people who worked at the mine lived?

In time, towns were built in lots of different places. Many towns grew up in places where traders met to swap their goods. Others were built in places where people found precious metals, stones or fuels such as coal or oil.

Some towns were built in places with natural harbours, where goods could be moved in or out of the town by boat.

Towns also grew up along the roads, canals and railways which were built to connect places together.

This picture, which was painted in 1823, shows cattle waiting to be loaded on to a boat at a port.

How towns grow

Do you know how old your town is? Can you find out why people first settled in your area? Your local library or museum should have records of the area in the past. Street names or old signs on buildings will also give you clues to how buildings were used in the past.

Look carefully at these three pictures. Can you see a reason why people settled in these places?

(The answers are at the bottom of the page.)

Answers:

1 Land good for farming

2 Coal found under the ground

3 Good place for crossing river

Today, we still need to build new towns to make room for more people. New towns are carefully planned to provide people with all the things they need, such as workplaces, leisure facilities, schools and shops.

Look carefully at this map of a new town called Haybridge.

Imagine you are the editor of a newspaper to advertise the town. What would you tell people about it? Look at the key on the map to find out about all the things there are to do in Haybridge.

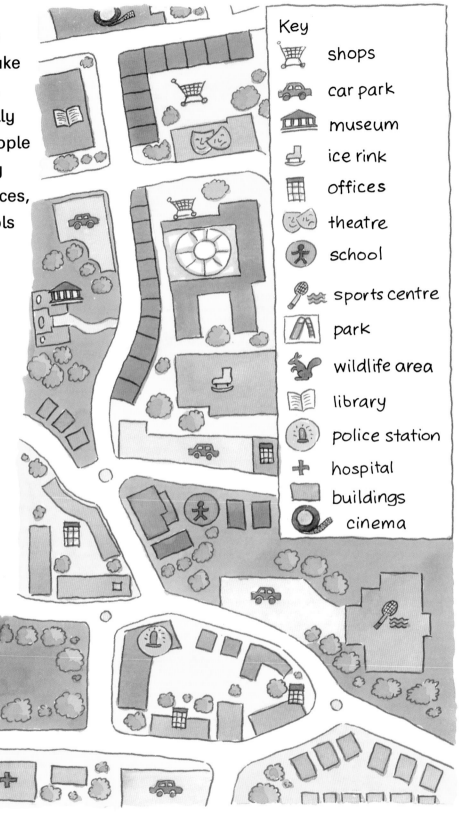

Key

shops

car park

museum

ice rink

offices

theatre

school

sports centre

park

wildlife area

library

police station

hospital

buildings

cinema

Look at these photographs of cities around the world. See if you can find the cities on a map. Why do you think they have grown into such big places?

Most towns and cities were once small villages. These villages grew as people moved there to look for work, and new houses, shops and leisure facilities had to be built to meet their needs.

Cape Town is on the south-western tip of South Africa. It has a population of 2 million people.

San Francisco, on the west coast of the USA, grew up as a gold rush town in the 1850s. Today 6 million people live there.

Bangkok, the capital of Thailand, was once a small fishing village on the Chao Phraya River. Today, nearly 6 million people live there.

Today, many cities are still growing and some are very overcrowded. Lots of the people who move to cities in search of work, money and a better life for their family, do not find it. Many are forced to live in shanty towns on the edge of cities, and to build their own homes out of scrap materials. Often there is no clean water, and germs and diseases spread quickly.

Sao Paulo, in Brazil, has a modern city centre surrounded by shanty towns. It has a population of over 10 million people.

Sometimes, whole refugee cities are set up to provide homes for people who have had to leave their own homes in a hurry. They may be running away from a war or a natural disaster such as an earthquake or a flood.

This refugee camp is on the border between Rwanda and Zaire.
The Rwandan refugees have had to leave their homes because of a war.

How a town works

In some small villages, such as this one in India, people grow their own food, fetch their own water and get rid of their own rubbish.

Meralaghatta, India

Most towns, however, employ a team of people, called a town council, to help the town run smoothly. They make sure that the town is provided with all the services it needs, such as schools, libraries, hospitals, refuse collection, public transport, a police force and a fire service.

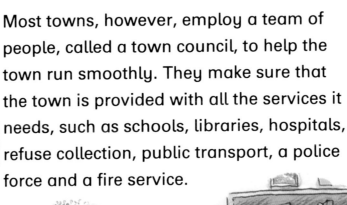

Towns need businesses too, such as banks, restaurants, shops and factories to provide work for people. They also need a good road and railway network to deliver food and materials to the town and take away finished goods.

This lorry is delivering goods to a shop in Sri Lanka.

Find out about the services that your town provides, the businesses in the town and the goods that go in and out of your local area. See if you can draw a plan of your town to show what you find out.

Choosing where to live

In the past, it was difficult for people to travel to other towns or villages and most people lived and worked in the same place. Nowadays, travelling from one place to another is much easier and people have more choice about where they live.

I live on the outskirts of a city. Dad and I can walk to our local football ground.

I live in a small village. At the weekend we drive to the nearest town to do the shopping.

I live in a big town. My sister and I go to the library on the bus.

Lots of people enjoy living in a busy town or city where they are close to their workplace and the facilities they need. But living in the middle of a city can be expensive and noisy, and the homes are often small and close together.

Some people live in suburbs on the outskirts of big towns. They can still get into town to use all the facilities, but their home area is much quieter.

Many people prefer to live in the countryside, away from crowded streets and noisy traffic, but they often have to spend a lot of time travelling to and from work. They also have to travel to nearby towns to use the facilities. As there's more open space in the countryside, homes are often larger with bigger gardens.

These houses have been divided into flats to make space for more people.

Commuters waiting for a train.

Ten minutes drive to supermarket

Good local bus service

Hour's drive to seaside resort

Village shop and post office

Lots of country walks

If someone was planning to move to your town or village, what useful things could you tell them about the area? Here are some ideas. What else can you think of?

Jobs

The jobs that people do often depend on where they live. In the countryside, many people have jobs to do with the land, such as ploughing fields and looking after animals.

A sheep farmer in Kent.

People who live near a town or city have a wider variety of jobs to choose from. They might work in hospitals, offices, shops, factories or restaurants. Lots of these jobs are done at different times of the day and night.

A motorbike courier in London.

Some people do the same kind of job in a town as other people do in the countryside. Look carefully at the people below. Who works in the countryside and who works in a town? Who could work in either place?

(The answers are at the bottom of the page.)

Answers:

Town = banker and nurse   Countryside = farmer   Either place = builder and postwoman

20

Journeys

What kind of journeys do you make each week? How long does it take you to get to places? If you live in the countryside, you may need to catch a bus to school or go in the car to the shops.

If you live in a town or city, you can probably walk to lots of places.
The roads are much busier than in the countryside and often vehicles are held up in traffic jams.

Dino has to deliver bread to these four restaurants early in the morning.

Which is the best route for him to take from the bread factory? The road outside the school is very busy, and there are road works near the swimming pool.

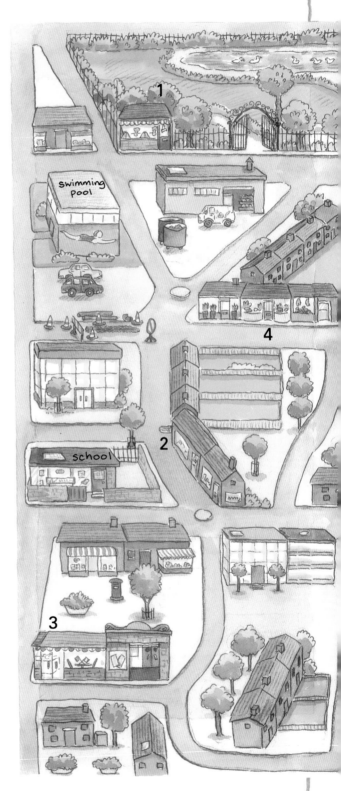

Planning towns and cities

Imagine you have just discovered this large island.
At the moment, no one lives here. The plan shows
where there are rivers, hills, valleys, flat land,
forests and animals. In the north of the
island the soil is good for farming,
and in the east, there is copper
under the ground. The cold
sea around the island
has plenty of fish.

N

Draw a plan of the island like the one shown here. Decide where are the best places to build small villages, towns and a city, and draw them on to your plan. It might be a good idea to build a city in a safe place which you could defend easily if the island was attacked.

Think about the shape of the land and how the people would get the goods and services they need. Where would you build roads and railways to link the places together? Where would be a good place to build a harbour so that goods could be taken to and from the island by ship? You need to make sure that your plan doesn't spoil too much of the countryside or destroy areas where animals live.

23

Changing the environment

Wherever people live, they cause problems for the environment. Homes, factories and offices use up huge amounts of energy and produce lots of waste. Vehicles and power stations give off poisonous fumes which pollute the air and water.

The more people that live in an area, the greater the problems are. One of the biggest problems in towns and cities is air pollution. Many places now have schemes to make the air cleaner.

Cycle lanes make it easier and safer for people to use bicycles instead of cars and buses.

In Mexico City, only certain cars are allowed into the city on certain days.

In the countryside, there are fewer people, buildings and vehicles polluting the air. But as towns and cities grow, they expand into the countryside and often cause damage to the environment. This expansion can also destroy the homes of wild animals, although some animals have adapted to living in city areas.

In India, there are more monkeys living in cities than in the forests.

Whether you live in a town or in the countryside, there are lots of things you can do to help the environment. Here are some ideas.

Use public transport where possible

Don't disturb birds or animals

Join a conservation group

Recycle glass, paper and tins

Use products made from recycled paper

Don't leave the taps dripping

Turn off lights

Take litter home with you

Cities of the future

Every year, the number of people living in the world increases. Many towns and cities are becoming overcrowded and there aren't enough homes, jobs and food for everyone.

These homeless people live on the streets in Bombay, India.

In 1960, a whole new capital city, Brasilia, was built to solve the problems of overcrowding in Rio de Janeiro, Brazil's old capital.

In the past when cities became overcrowded, new towns were built. In the future there will be less space to build new towns. People may have to live in hot deserts or icy lands and spend more time indoors where they can control things like heating and lighting.

Some countries have already built artificial islands and others are planning whole cities underground or under the sea.

This island is called Foueda. It is one of a group of artificial islands. which have been built in Lau Lagoon in the Solomon Islands.

If you were building a new city on Earth, where would you build it? You need to think about how people would travel to and from the city and how they would get the goods and services they need. See if you can draw a picture of your imaginary city. Would you like to live in a place like this one day?

Index

For parents and teachers
More about the ideas in this book

Pages 6/9 Encourage the children to consider the similarities and differences between living in a village, a town and a city. Think about things such as their size, schools, jobs, transport, housing, shops, leisure activities and pollution problems.

Pages 10/15 About 10,000 years ago, people stopped being hunter-gatherers and settled down to become farmers. The earliest settlements were places with a good water supply, a warm climate, a safe defensive position, rich farmland and rivers or harbours for travel and trade.

Pages 16/17 City dwellers rely a great deal on the goods and services provided by other people. Rules and regulations ensure cities function efficiently, but often, people do not have a say in the way things are run. In the countryside, people have more opportunity to take part in local decision-making.

Pages 18/19 Many people choose to live in an area of countryside near to a town, called the catchment area, so that they can live in quiet surroundings, but still make use of all the town's facilities.

Page 20 In developed countries, many of the jobs that people did in the countryside are now being done by machines. Work in the countryside is influenced by the weather, climate and seasons.

Page 21 In the countryside, there is less public transport, but the roads aren't as crowded and polluted as they are in towns and cities.

Pages 22/23 In planning a new town, factors such as landscape, drainage, local materials and transport links all have to be considered. The position of other towns and villages and the location of jobs in the area are also important.

Pages 24/25 Encourage the children to find out about ways of making their own environment 'greener', such as tree planting, increasing public transport, and re-routing traffic out of villages.

Pages 26/27 Due to new technology, cities of the future could be built in places previously considered uninhabitable, such as Antarctica.

...hings to do

...**...ing places** provides starting points for ... kinds of cross-curricular work based on ...ography and the environment, looking at ...ur locality and at the wider world.

...**...wn and countryside** explores the growth ... settlements and looks at similarities and ...fferences between villages, towns and cities, ...vestigating how land and buildings are ...ed and the impact of settlements on the ...vironment. Here are some suggestions for ...llow-up activities to extend the ideas further.

...Children could take a closer look at maps ...d aerial photographs of their local area ... see how the shape of villages and towns ...ries. Some housing is scattered across the ...untryside, while some is concentrated ...gether in tight groups called 'nuclear' ...ttlements. If the housing is spread out along ...e sides of roads or rivers, this is called a ...near or a ribbon development. Medieval ...wns often had walls around them.

...Making a scale model of an imaginary ...wn is a good way of getting children to ...ppreciate all the different elements of a town ...d how they fit together. The children could ...aw a land-use map of their model town, ...ing different colour codes for things like ...ops, houses and offices.

...Go on a sound journey in the local area. ...he children could draw a sketch map and ...ark on where they noticed each different ...ise.

...The first cities were built about 5000 years ...go in the Middle East. Encourage the ...ildren to find out about ancient cities, such ... Jericho, Mohenjo-daro in Pakistan and ...ncient Egyptian cities along the river Nile. ...Vhy did the cities grow up? What sort of ...ouses did the people live in? What crops did ...ey grow? Did they trade goods with ...her areas?

...Drama activities could be developed from ...e jobs of a town council. For example, the children could take turns at being the council member in charge of leisure facilities who has to deal with residents who are angry at the closure of the local swimming pool.

6 Find out about some of the many animals that have adapted to life in cities. Bats that used to live in caves now shelter in attics and towers. Pigeons and kestrels nest on building ledges instead of the cliffs of their natural homes. Storks nest on chimneys instead of tall trees and foxes, racoons, kites and gulls scavenge for our left-over food scraps.

7 Make a scrapbook of ten cities around the world, such as New York, Mexico City, Delhi, Nairobi, London, Moscow, Cairo, Shanghai, Tokyo and Sydney. How old is each city? How many people live there? About 9 million people live in Cairo, while in Mexico City, the population is expected to reach 31 million by the year 2000. Why did the cities grow up? What sort of jobs do the people do? Are there any traffic or pollution problems? What sort of climate does the city have?

8 Write a story about setting up a new town. How did you decide where to build the town? Is it near to a big city? What jobs are people going to do? How could you make your town a pollution-free environment?

9 Make a jigsaw of a countryside scene, such as a farmyard, a holiday village, wildlife park, mountain rescue or hiking centre.

10 Visit a local village, or another part of a town, and carry out a survey to answer questions such as: How are the buildings used? How has the function of the buildings changed over the years? What are the biggest buildings used for? Are buildings with the same uses found on the same street?

11 Arrange real pen friends for the children by contacting a school in another county. If your town is twinned with a town abroad, you may be able to link up with a school there.